ARTIST'S EASEL

Alma Flor Ada
F. Isabel Campoy

ALFAGUARA
YOUNG READERS
SANTILLANA

Originally published in Spanish as *Caballete*

Art Director: Felipe Dávalos
Design: Arroyo + Cerda S.C.
Editor: Norman Duarte

Cover: Simón Silva, *Two Women*

Text © 2000 Alma Flor Ada and F. Isabel Campoy
Edition © 2000 Santillana USA Publishing Company, Inc.

Santillana USA Publishing Company, Inc.
2105 NW 86th Avenue
Miami, FL 33122

The authors gratefully acknowledge the editorial assistance
of Debra Luna.

Art C: *Artist's Easel*

ISBN: 1-58105-576-5

Printed in Colombia
Panamericana Formas e Impresos S.A.

To our fathers, Modesto and Diego,
who gave things their names.

To Be Yourself

How beautiful
to be who you are,
to look at yourself straight in the eye,
to see the sun in your own heart,
to color your pride
slowly, bit by bit.

How beautiful
to see yourself as you are.
What a joy it is!

Shining Light
Maya Christina González

With just a pen
and a bottle of ink,
an artist can capture
all the world's wonder.

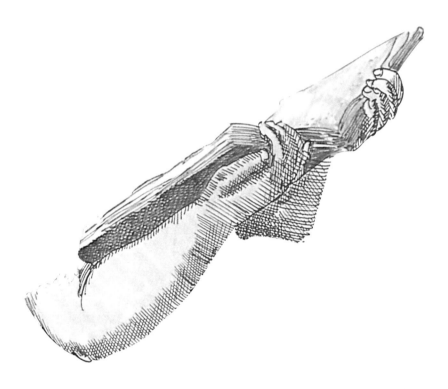

Little Girl Reading
José Giménez and José Massi

I see,
I think,
I understand.
I love to read.

6

First you take some paper
and then paint with oils
shapes, lines, and color,
pictures to hang on your wall.

Fried Omelette, Goldie Yolk, and *Merry White*
Raymond Ezra

You draw,
you paint,
you make things prettier.
You like to play and create.

Paper, brush, and pen
there's a goat again.
It looks up above
and smiles back with love.

Goat Looking at the Sky
Francisco Álvarez

Think,
imagine,
dream.
You love to play and invent.

45/50   F. ALVAREZ

Matadors and traditions,
suits full of light.
There come the musicians;
it's time for the bullfight.

Family Scene
Fernando Botero

Our clothes
and our shoes
can be works of art.
A person with a skill and a craft
is also an artist.

O ff in the distance
wolves howl at the moon,
but here near the town
there's a great big balloon.

The Balloon
Ramón Cano

 They help,
they laugh,
they play.
They dream of flying some day.

You look and then ever closer.

What can it be?

What is it that is there?

It's like love and like care;

you cannot see them,

but you feel that they're there.

The Skiing Lesson
Joan Miró

They try,
they fall,
and again they try.
They all love to ski!

In the sky shines a moon
and a thousand bright stars.
A plane, swooping down,
almost hits the little town.

Accident
Rodolfo Morales

With paper and scissors
you can make pictures,
with cut-out hearts
and cut-out faces.

The sunflowers turn
their great faces with care,
so they can see the women
who are washing their hair.

The sunflowers wish
for petals long and lank,
so they can wash their petals
in a tub or in a tank.

Two Women
Simón Silva

Happiness and brush strokes
create flowers
the color of honey.

The painter paints a portrait,
a portrait of her,
right under the tree,
just where he met her.

The Girl and the Flame Tree
Antonio Martorell

A portrait
gives us a face
and, in it,
a heart.

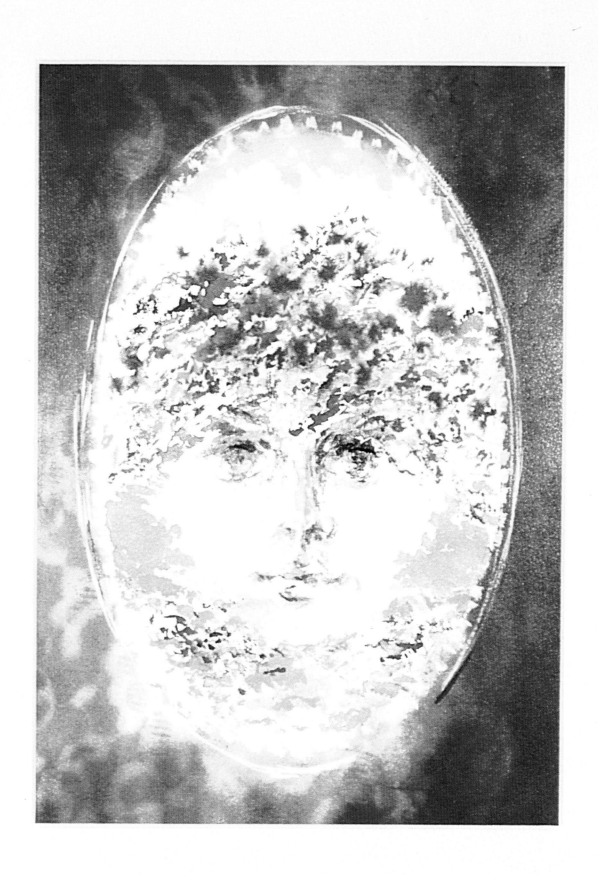

A family portrait,
the family of a king,
done by a great artist,
with brush, paint, and canvas.

The Family of Carlos IV
Francisco de Goya

Paint your own family portrait.
Yours is also the family of royalty,
and you are the highest rank
of nobility.

⬤⬥ Maya Christina González

Maya Christina González was born in Lancaster, California, in 1964. She is a painter and graphic artist as well as an illustrator of children's books. Her work appears in international magazines, and her paintings form part of several private collections. She lives in San Francisco.

Shining Light

⬤⬥ Painting herself, the artist wanted to show the light that shines from her heart. To adorn herself, she put pencils and brushes in her hair. It is an expressionist painting full of color.

⬤⬥ José Giménez

This nineteenth-century painter and graphic artist illustrated many children's books and posters. He favored ink and pen to create realistic scenes.

Little Girl Reading

⬤⬥ The peace captured in this drawing invites us to read. The eyes of the spectator want to read the book and know more about where the girl is. The whiteness of the page invites us to come closer. It is a woodblock print.

➤ RAYMOND EZRA

Raymond Ezra is a Spanish painter who reflects life around him with charm and innocence. His art shows his warm feeling towards the landscape and the people of his town, Medinacelli, in the province of Soria, Spain.

Fried Omelette, Goldie Yolk, and Merry White

➤ These characters are caricatures of three people in any small town. The background landscapes are different but similar. The detail with which this painter covers the canvas gives the viewer a realistic sense of the atmosphere of the place and motivates us to know more about his characters. They are done in an expressionistic style.

➤ FRANCISCO ÁLVAREZ

This outstanding Spanish painter utilizes mixed media to express his creativity. He paints with oil, does silkscreen prints, and illustrates books. The originality of his imagination is stimulating. He lives in Madrid. His wife, Viví Escrivá, and daughters, Ana and Sandra López Escrivá, are also well-known painters.

Goat Looking at the Sky

➤ A fence encloses this goat in its pen, but its eyes are open to the sky and its imagination. This is an aquatint etching.

❧ FERNANDO BOTERO

Fernando Botero was born in Medellín, Colombia, in 1932. Early in his life he began to study the classical painters. He studied in Spain, Italy, and France. Many of his paintings are re-creations of famous paintings, such as the *Mona Lisa*. Monumentality is the salient characteristic of his work, both in painting and sculpture. He is a world-renowned artist.

Family Scene

❧ The tradition of bullfighting is still maintained in Latin American countries and in Spain. Fernando Botero paints bullfighting scenes often. He learned to love bullfights as a child when he frequented them with his uncle. This work is in oils on canvas.

❧ RAMÓN CANO

Ramón Cano was born in Mexico in 1888. He belonged to the neo-impressionist school of painting. He was interested in reflecting people and the everyday life around him. He became the Director of the Open Air Academy of Art in Coyoacán. He died in 1974.

The Balloon

❧ As a member of the Open Air school, Ramón would set up his easel near parks or on the streets of his town. He painted whatever he saw happening. On this particular Sunday afternoon, people admire how a hot-air balloon takes flight. It is a neo-impressionist painting.

JOAN MIRÓ

Joan Miró was born in Catalonia, Spain, in 1893. Miró is one of the foremost artists of the twentieth century. He studied at the Academy of Art in Barcelona and later traveled to Paris, where he became acquainted with the new styles that were breaking with the realistic fashion of the past. Besotted with color, he joins bold splotches with heavy black lines to create an atmosphere of innocence and poetry.

The Skiing Lesson

The painting is filled with circles, squares, and rectangles of color, joined by black slashes and totemic symbols. Imagination does the interpretation. The title that the painter has chosen drives us towards the backdrop of white. This surrealist painting invites us to enjoy color without form.

RODOLFO MORALES

Rodolfo Morales was born in Oaxaca, Mexico, in 1925. He grew up surrounded by color—in the fields, in the special clothes worn at festivals, and in traditional paper cut-outs. Contrast abounds in his compositions, in which he uses different materials in his collages with paint and drawing superimposed.

Accident

Rodolfo Morales describes this painting by telling how one day an American pilot made a forced landing behind the town's cemetery. It caused a big commotion in the town. The painter is in the bottom left corner. It is an expressionist painting.

SIMÓN SILVA

Simón Silva was born in 1962 in Mexicali, Mexico, and grew up in Holtville, California. As a child he felt a special calling to painting, and he often reproduced the color of the fields where he and his family were farm workers. Self-taught, Simón's paintings reflect the life and culture of the Latino people, showing pride and deep respect for his roots.

Two Women

The sunflower dances around the sun and at dusk it bows its head waiting for a new day. Two women bend to wash their hair after a day of work under the sun. Light fills every inch of the painting. It is a collage.

ANTONIO MARTORELL

Antonio Martorell is one of the best-known Puerto Rican painters. He has exhibited internationally. He has had both one-man and group exhibits abroad. His versatility is reflected by the wide range of media he uses. He is also active in theater, film, dance, and poetry recitals.

The Girl and the Flame Tree

The outline of a flame tree frames the face of a girl who, under its branches, remembers her past. This painting was created for the cover of a book of childhood memories entitled *Where the Flame Trees Bloom,* written by Alma Flor Ada.

☙❖ FRANCISCO DE GOYA

Francisco de Goya was born in Zaragoza, Spain, in 1746. He was the painter of the court of Carlos IV, but he also painted the life and customs of the people of Madrid. Because of the broad spectrum of themes depicted in his painting and his sense of color and attention to detail, he is considered one of the masters of Spanish painting. He died in 1828.

The Family of Carlos IV

☙❖ This realistic painting pays exquisite attention to detail in the clothes, gestures, faces, and composition. It is one of the best-known masterpieces of Spanish painting. Here King Carlos IV appears surrounded by all his family.

ACKNOWLEDGEMENTS

Cover; page 21 / Simón Silva, *Two Women.* Copyright © 1991 Simón Silva. Reproduction authorized by Simón Silva and BookStop Literary Agency.

Page 5 / Maya Christina González, *Shining Light.* Copyright © 1997 Maya Christina González. From *Just Like Me,* edited by Harriet Rohmer. Children´s Book Press, San Francisco, CA. Reprinted with permission of the publisher.

Page 7 / *Little Girl Reading,* drawing by José Giménez, engraving by José Massi del Castillo. From *Libro de estampas: Almanaque de los niños 1800-1892* by Ana Pelegrín. Comunidad de Madrid, Consejería de Educación, Dirección General de Educación / Madrid, Spain, 1989. Reproduction authorized by Ana Pelegrín.

Page 9 / Raymond Ezra, *Fried Omelette, Goldie Yolk,* and *Merry White.* Copyright © Raymond Ezra. Reproduction authorized by the artist.

Page 11 / Francisco Álvarez, *Goat Looking at the Sky.* Copyright © Francisco Álvarez. Reproduction authorized by the artist.

Page 13 / Fernando Botero, *Family Scene.* Copyright © Fernando Botero, *Family Scene*, 1985, courtesy of Marlborough Gallery, New York.

Page 15 / Ramón Cano, *The Balloon.* Copyright © 2000 Consejo Nacional para la Cultura y las Artes / Instituto Nacional de Bellas Artes y Literatura / Museo Nacional de Arte / Mexico.

Page 17 / Joan Miró, *The Skiing Lesson,* 1966. Copyright © 2000 Artists Rights Society (ARS), New York / ADAGP, Paris and Museo de Arte Contemporáneo de Caracas Sofía Imber. Reproduction authorized by ARS and the Museo de Arte Contemporáneo de Caracas.

Page 19 / Rodolfo Morales, *Accident.* Copyright © 1997 Rodolfo Morales. From *Just Like Me,* edited by Harriet Rohmer. Children's Book Press, San Francisco, CA. Reproduction authorized by the publisher.

Page 23 / Antonio Martorell, *The Girl and the Flame Tree.* From the private collection of Alma Flor Ada.